VENTURING VULNERABILITY

Jessika Bertrand

BookLeaf Publishing

India | USA | UK

Presentation by BookLeaf Publishing

Web: www.bookleafpub.com

E-mail: info@bookleafpub.com

ISBN: 9789358362183

First edition 2021

TO THOSE BRAVE ENOUGH TO FALL IN LOVE

PREFACE

"I believe that everything happens for a reason. People change so that you can learn to let go, things go wrong so that you appreciate them when they're right, you believe lies so you eventually learn to trust no one but yourself, and sometimes good things fall apart so better things can fall together."

– Marilyn Monroe

SELF-PORTRAIT

I was late to class

Running up the creaky stairs,

Everyone was waiting

With their ugly, judgmental stares.

Sunlight shone through the spotty,

8-paned window

And particles danced like fireflies

In this old, dusty studio.

I quickly found my empty canvas

And stood to look at you:

My guide, my muse, my inspiration.

You instructed us on what to do:

A simple task, you told the group,

A portrait of your truest self

The fire that burns within your soul

Truer than the mirror itself.

The eager learners set off at once,

Purples and yellows and pinks and blue

Swishing, dipping and dabbing away.

I stood there motionless, like I didn't have a clue.

I held the paintbrush in my hand

Dripping with my shade of hazel

But the canvas felt too formal,

My truest self was not so simple.

I looked up and found my eyes in yours

And in that moment, realized

That it was you. That in your presence,

My truest self was undisguised.

It was you that was my canvas,

That saw all of my shades and colours

And I saw yours too, reflected,

Infinite rainbows and endless summers.

You are the yellow burst of sunshine

That brightens my day,

The red hot love

That fills my veins in every way.

The blazing wildfire

That sparks my thoughts, awakens me

And the royal purple that reminds me

That yes, I am worthy.

You are the playful bubblegum kisses

That colour my cheeks in pink

And the depth of the bluest oceans

That challenges me, makes me think.

I looked around at the others

Painting within the lines of the predetermined canvas

And I dipped my fingers into the cool paint and decided

I shall not be so anonymous.

And so I went to you

And ran my fingers down your face.

Purple, yellow, blue and more,

So that every colour had its place.

You took my rainbow hands in yours

And smiled to my soul,

Then grabbed my face and kissed it

And for a moment I was whole.

My portrait is yours, it's mine,

It's nothing like the others.

I am sorry I was late

But these are my truest colours.

BEAUTY IN ME

Some days, I seem to lose myself

Unsure of who I am

My strength

My resilience

My charm

Simple fragments of a long-lost self

A simpler life that knew no harm

But you put the pain

Back into place

Reminded me

That the ache

Isn't who I am

I'd grown used to the mask of agony

Truly, I've got but myself to blame

You made giving up

A foreign thought

Forcing me

To see myself

Through your eyes

Showing me beauty I never dared to see

Making me believe. Helping me realize

You see the light

That is inside

Of me

A uniqueness

That nobody else could define

No need to hide behind a mask of woes

Beauty through your eyes and mine

LOST IN YOU

Basking in the beauty, falling deeper

Into the meadow of your mind,

A gentle breeze through my hair

I feel your skin as it grazes mine.

Unwinding, wrapped in your love

Tranquility fills my soul,

Getting lost in you

I have never felt so whole.

This grasp you have

Python hug holding tight

Never let it weaken, love,

Nothing has ever felt so right.

RAPTURE

Golden and refined

A honeyed mirage

Forged,

Not mine.

I want it raw,

Unfiltered.

Give me that...

Set your soul on fire

Kind of love.

Give me

Life...

Immortality.

INAMORATO

Falling to places

Most unknown,

The beaten path a distant memory

Forged by the love it sows.

Undistinguishable

Normal perhaps.

Like his

Like hers.

Trained to want this,

Desire the mediocre,

Conventional…known and safe.

But this…

It is nameless

Ours,

Shall we not strive for greatness?

Unplanned

Shattering molds

Adventitious

Discovery filled with trepidation.

My mind is charged

Ignited by the thought of you,

Do we dare to be fearless?

To be exceptional?

INAMORATA

Foolish girl

To believe the fabrications

Of his words.

Did you really trust that it was greatness?

That you were special?

It was nothing but lust

Set firmly between his legs

That coveted you,

Attempting to access the deepest corners

Of your mind.

A ruse.

The greatest magic trick.

It is not your beauty,

Your thoughts,

Or your strength

But rather

Your credulity

That won him over.

The depth, a mirage

A fragility

Of the mind.

LIMERENCE

Meeting you, our souls collide

Everything fits, worlds align

The perfect match

It's yours. It's mine.

You're the coffee on my lips

The energy runs through me;

It's warm, you are golden

Glowing for the world to see.

You are vivid and dazzling,

You have grown so bright

Stepping back, I shield my eyes

Stunning beauty of your light.

The power of your spark

Mine flickers and I fade,

Shockwaves to my soul

What is this that we have made?

This is love...right? This is it?

Eagerly watching with bated breath

But instead, you rise

Upon the pedestal that I created.

I look up to find you,

Craning my neck to see

But you are not the one who is rising,

I am the one that is shrinking. It's me.

Everything you do is golden, Midas perhaps?

Will you touch me too?

Please don't leave me behind.

Make me beautiful too.

MAKE HASTE

Down by the shed,

The creaky one, remember?

My face freckled by the sun.

I handed you a shovel

And we began to dig

Little homes for

Raspberry bushes.

Day by day,

Watered by our love

They grew and grew

Until little green berries

Began to appear

But your happiness

Faded to greed

As you plucked

The berries

From their home.

I tried to stop you.

Edacious,

You took them whole.

Your face

Contorted.

Bitter on your tongue,

You spat at my feet

And I wanted to yell

I told you so

But you were already gone,

Never quite the patient one

And now you'll never know

The bliss

Of a raspberry whole.

INNOCENCE

You held out your hands to me

And swept me off my feet;

You promised me the world

You were the man I longed to meet.

Building up our empire

Meticulous, brick by brick

We were the untouchables

Impenetrable, our walls so thick.

I never noticed the feeble door,

The Achilles' heel to our love:

You left it open for all to enter

My flattery alone was not enough

I lay oblivious upon a bed of roses

Confusing the thorns digging deep

For a love I was so convinced of.

You were the man I wanted to keep.

But you were never mine

And this castle was never ours;

You built it with the bricks of other girls

Enchanted by their pretty flowers.

Heart beating in a frantic panic

As I finally saw the truth before me,

I ran from your collapsing towers

Leaving my innocence in the debris.

SAFE SPACE

You opened your arms

And wrapped me in,

Like hot cocoa on a Winter's Day.

My heart cocooned inside the warmth of you.

My protector.

My guards down in your safety.

My love grew and lifted me to the skies,

Soaring higher and higher.

I didn't see you run.

You were not there to catch me as I fell.

It wasn't the broken bones

That damaged me,

It was the emptiness.

Vulnerable,

Naked and exposed.

Limb by limb,

I scraped myself from the ground.

It seemed impossible, but I did it.

I thought I'd be stronger.

That's what they all said.

I didn't believe them,

So brick by brick,

I built a wall around me.

Then I reinforced it,

So that nobody could get in.

Fortified.

Ready for the wrath of love.

ONSRA

You played in the sandbox

Basking in the golden sun

With my shovel and my bucket.

I asked if I could join the fun.

You smiled as I sat to join you;

The warm sand between my toes

Your sunkissed knee on mine

And freckles on your nose.

You showed me to your pride and joy

A sandcastle built with love

Every door, every side, every angle,

Even the view from up above.

I oohed and ahhed at you

As you beamed at me with delight.

"Let's build one together," I suggested,

But your smile turned to fright.

I cannot build castles with you,

You whispered to the air

And left me sitting all alone,

Sand still dripping from my hair.

IT MIGHT HAVE BEEN

I thought I lost you,

But you were never mine

False pretense

A bandaid for your time.

My love, I gladly gave

Grabbing hastily to ease the pain

I soothed your aching heart,

I thought maybe you'd do the same.

But you got your fill

And left me broken on the floor.

I thought you loved me,

We might have been so much more

BLACKOUT LOVE

The words bellowed through me

Like waves in the angry sea,

Touching every corner of my soul,

Staining the innocence of my being.

You kept falling under

Influenced by your state

Grasping,

Begging to take me with you.

Intoxicated by your words

I stumble,

Searching for my strength,

Searching your eyes

For the love I once knew.

Tears cloud my vision

And I cannot find you.

The poisonous sting of your voice

Echoes through my mind,

Swells inside of me,

Threatening to stay.

Gone.

You have been carried away

By your world,

A shadow

Of the man I love

Until daylight breaks

And you find the broken pieces

Of what's left of me,

Carefully gluing them back together.

Never quite the same.

Fused by apologies,

Sealed with a kiss

And a promise,

Until we break again.

MY INFECTION

The tears came

Threatening to explode.

Vision clouded

Drowning out my soul.

Standing helpless

Vulnerable

And

Exposed

I was an open wound.

You were my infection.

I scratched you out

Eager to be rid of you;

Oozing,

Staining my skin,

You returned

Reptilian.

The grace of time

Took you away,

Scales fading,

Forever tarnished

By scars of you.

ETCHED INTO ME

I made myself a promise

When you walked away from me

That I would forget you

And set myself completely free.

Still blazing through my veins,

I stopped wildfire at the source

Still… you're burning through me

And I don't know what is worse:

The pain and empty sorrow

of a love now lost

Or to never know what love is

To play it safe, no matter the cost.

AUGURI

It's in the stars

That shoot across the sky.

It's in the candles that flicker

On every birthday cake.

It's in the dandelion seeds

Blowing in the wind.

It's in the eyelash

Resting upon my cheek.

It's in the pot of gold

At the end of the rainbow.

It's in the time on the clock

When it strikes 11:11.

It's in the copper pennies

Splashing in fountains.

It's in the leaves

Falling to the ground.

It's in the moon

That guides me to you.

It's everywhere.

It's everything.

It's always you.

YOU

Bearing the mediocre,

Iron bars cannot hold our love.

It is air

It is water

It is inside and out

Ever present, a necessity

The understated beauty

Of simplicity.

Unbreakable, breaking free.

The caged bird sings

With sunlight upon its wings,

Tickled by clouds,

Dancing in the sky.

A realization sets in:

This is it.

The vitality of love.

EQUANIMITY

You're not just love

You're freedom

You're light

My inner voice

My thoughts

My anchor

Body

Mind

Soul

EVERY STORY HAS A COLOUR

Deep down into my soul

Your whispers flow right through me

Golden and mellifluous,

Your voice, it turns to honey.

It travels through my body

Places yet to be known;

You navigate right through them

To this space that's now your home.

You are searching endlessly,

Insatiable for more,

Staking an unwavering claim

And locking up the door.

It's an epoch in the making

The grandest of stories to be told.

Once upon a time? No, not this.

Fairytales are much too cold.

This is fire, eruption of the core.

It's painted in our eyes.

Words cannot describe

Ineffable, it's rated you and I.

UNCORKED

I brought you a bottle of wine,

Your kisses asked me to stay.

Yours, I whispered,

Always?

Always.